GOING BANANAS

My Family, Me, and our Chimpanzee

Marvin Ginsburg, M.D.

Illustrated by Ian McCartor

DEDICATION

To all my kids, my wife Marty, and grandson Blake.

Mark, Shane, Bruce, Norine, Carol, Susan, who all experienced the joys and the sorrows
of this life's rare event.

Blake only experienced our memories and stories
as he was not yet born.

This book is also dedicated to my daughter Carol who has left this world at a young age,
but will forever live in my heart.
She was also a champion of animal freedom and justice.

And

lovers of all animals throughout the whole world.

ACKNOWLEDGEMENTS

Stephanie Sotomayor, LVN, encouraged me to write this children's book after listening to the true story about my life living with a chimpanzee and my family.

Mason and Sophia Swenson, and their mother Traci, MBA.
This beautiful, intelligent family inspired me in seeing a need to inform little ones about wildlife issues, tragedies and happiness.

Jami Doran, LVN, and her baby Ema.
Jamie, now expecting her new baby that I hope to inform when both children are old enough to understand this book's discoveries that took me so many years to grasp.

Ian McCartor, my illustrator, whose artistic talent captured the emotions and feelings of my story. IanMcCartor.com

One day my wife said to me,
"Let's bring home a chimpanzee?"
I confessed that we could try.
She looked at me with a teary eye.

So, I called a well-known
chimp trainer,
who said that
he would help.

It couldn't have
been any plainer.
I thanked him
with a joyous yelp.

Soon thereafter,

I was rewarded.

I had the chimp in my car.

Heading home happy (sort of).

The drive wasn't all too far.

In my arms that little guy,
staring at me with a wonderous eye.
Opening my front door, and feeling so proud,
I heard my wife screaming aloud.

"Oh my God, Oh my God",
she cried with joy.

'A baby chimp, and he's a boy!
What shall we name him
by the way?"

I said,

"I know,
we'll call him
Joey!"

Touching her face with his small finger,

allowing it to pause and linger.

Giving her then a great big hug,
immediately showing he was a love bug.

He lived in our house.

And also outside.

Sometimes we took him
on a car ride.

We built a big, strong cage just for him,

where he could climb and swing within.

Problems arose when the horses came near,
Joey excited whether from fun or fear.
Throwing rocks and things that he dared,
to frighten them and make them scared.

In time he came to like the horse,
so my wife taught him to ride of course!

Then came a horse show
where my girls would ride.

Lo and behold she took Joey inside.

Western saddle
and child-sized boots,
he entered the ring
to hollers and hoots.

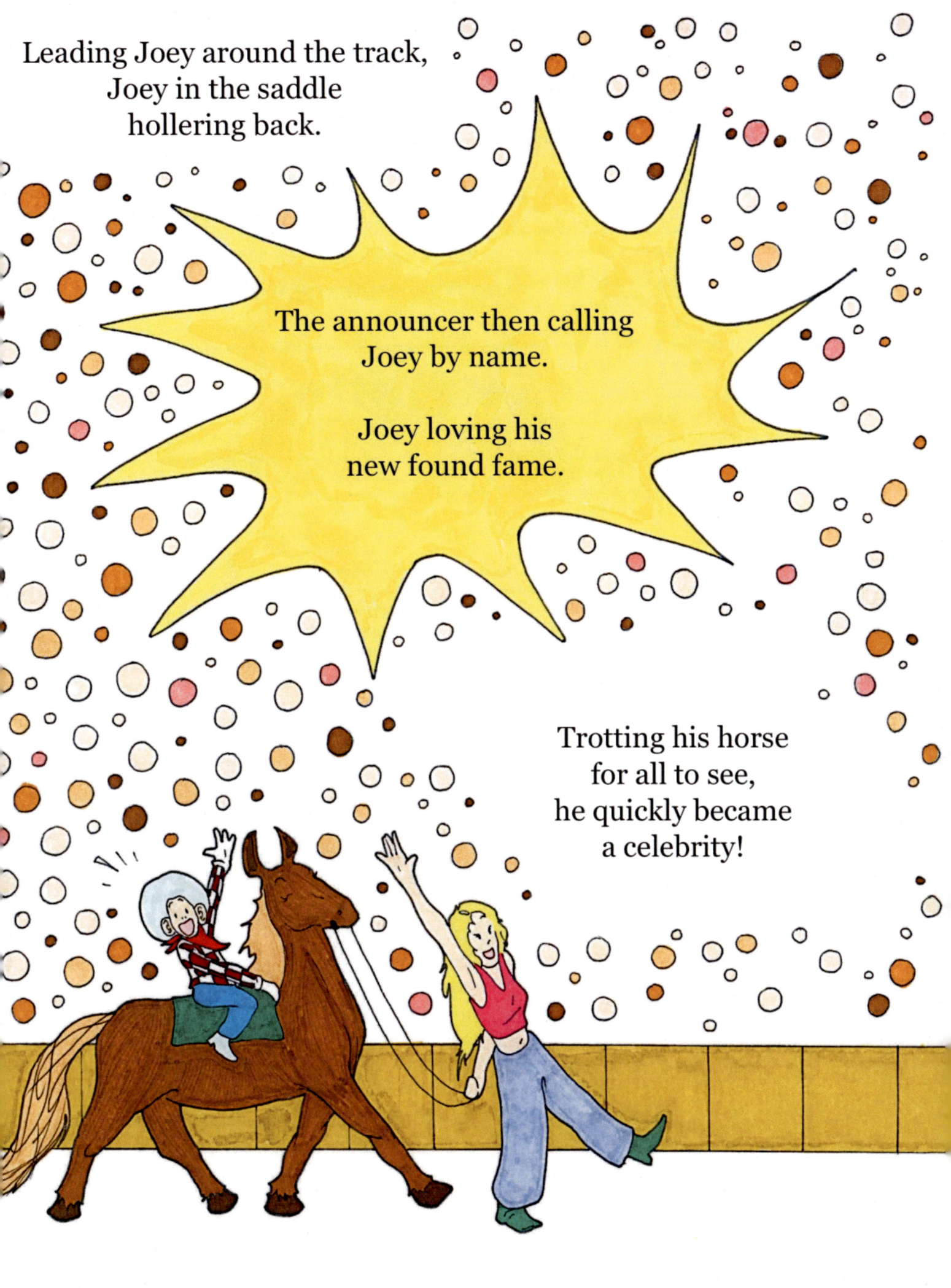

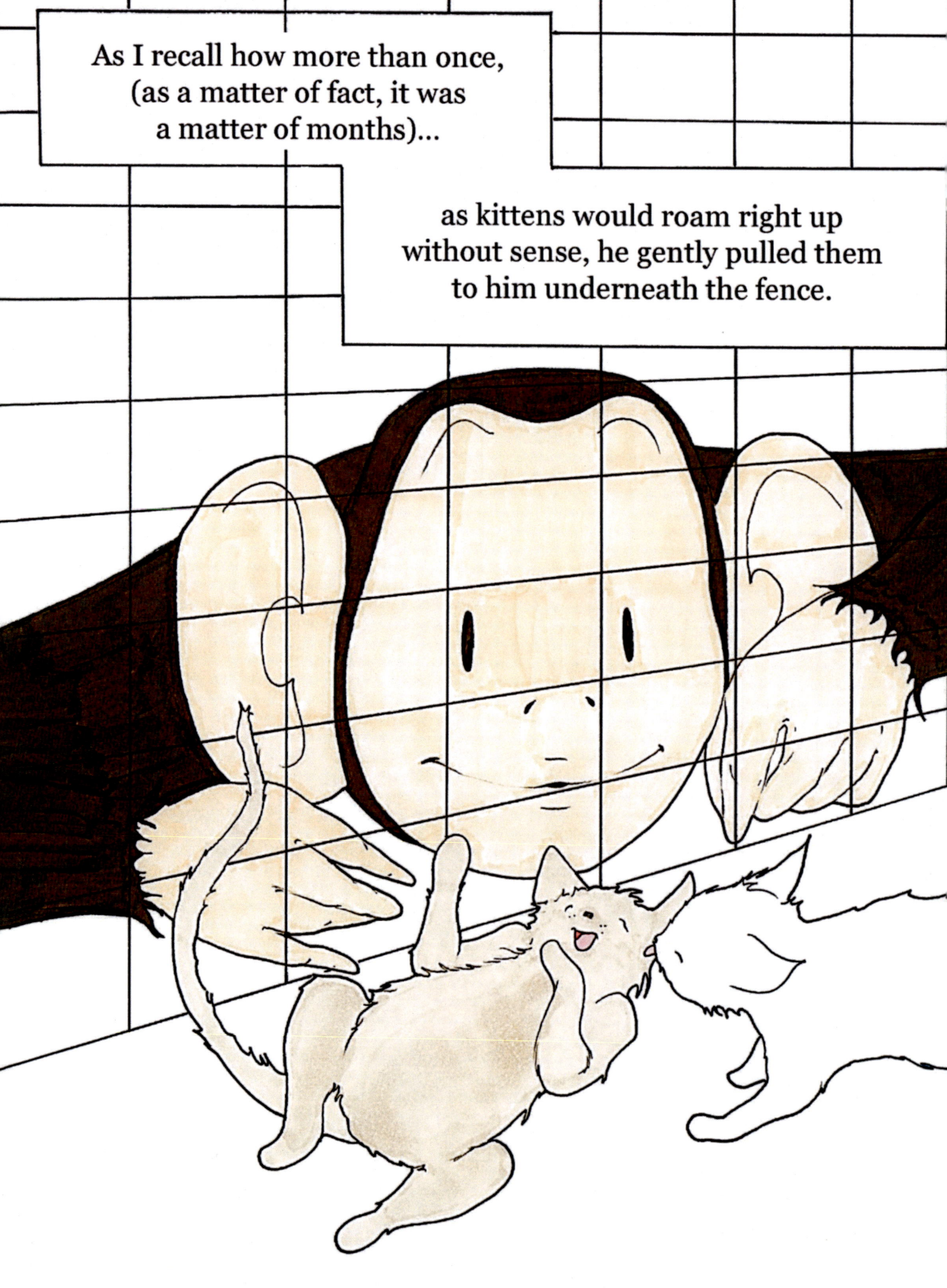

Joey carried them
up to his high place,
stroking and lifting them
to his face.

Loving the kittens just like a mother,
maybe he thought he was their brother.

The kittens adopted him with love.
He assumed they were a gift
from the good Lord above.

Once we went to Lake Havasu,
even took Joey along with us too.
He hated water, but we thought yet,
He should learn to swim,
(or at least get wet).

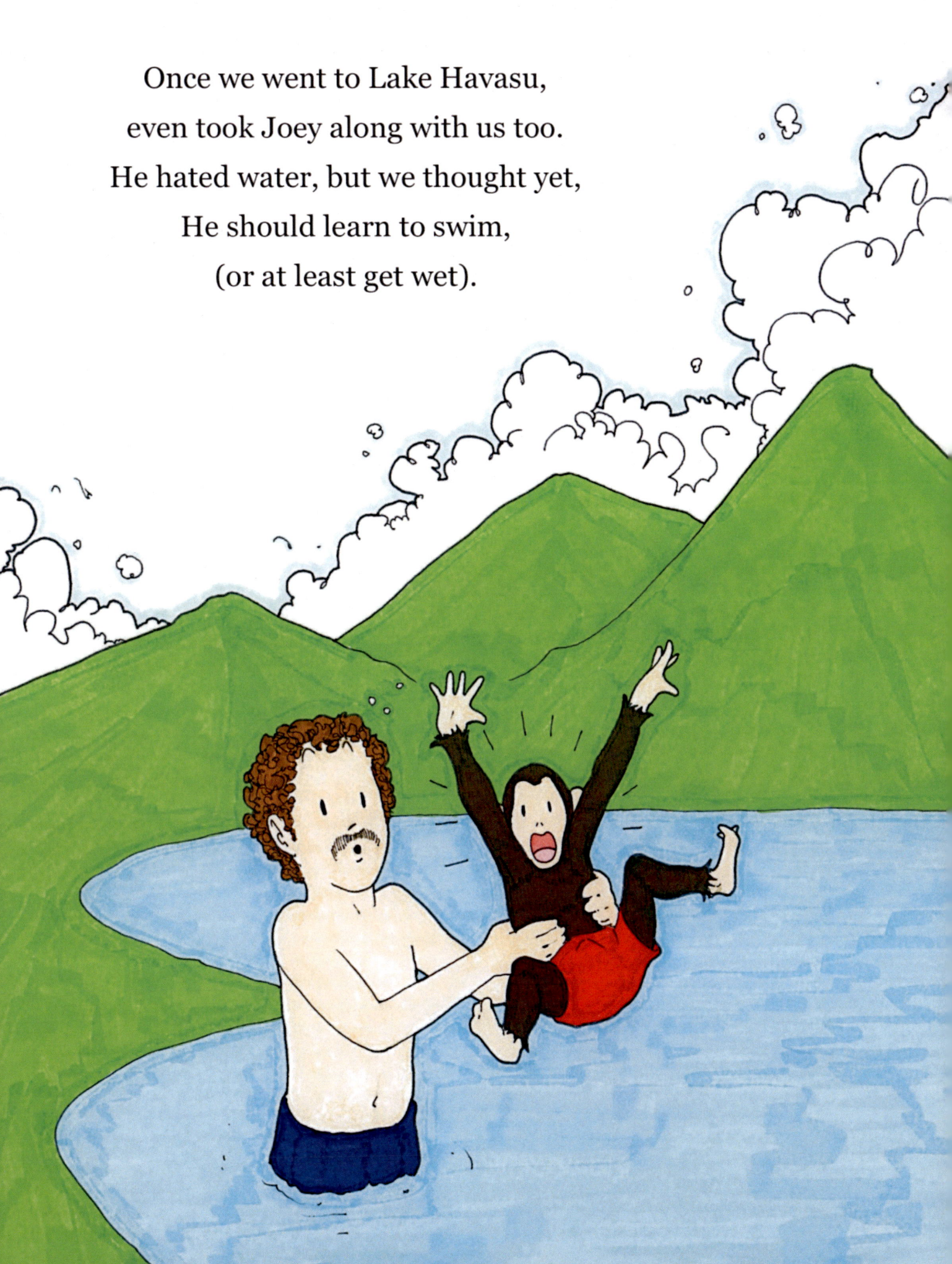

With four hands holding,
he got free.
Running like the wind
from my wife and me.

Up the palm tree
he did climb,

remaining there for
a very long time.

Throughout the night and into the morn,

finally coming down very forlorn.

I needed to teach him some good manners, I thought.

Nothing better

than using

bananas I bought.

He loved them,
so I'd been told.
I held two out
and he took hold.

Screaming at me to give another,
I gave him some more,
(five all together).

Tucking two under his neck,
looking around to count and check.
Two were now right in his hand,
but mine were now all in the sand.

Still unhappy, so he screamed again.
I offered two more to him,
and then...

Frustrated he was
that he could not eat
them all at once
(his favorite treat).

He threw them all onto the ground,
picking each up
and swallowing it down.
Continued to eat till he ate all nine.
Joey now happy and feeling fine.

One day the wife said to me,
"Why don't we take Joey out to ski?'
"Ski?" I said, "He'll hate the snow!"
It didn't matter,
what did we know?

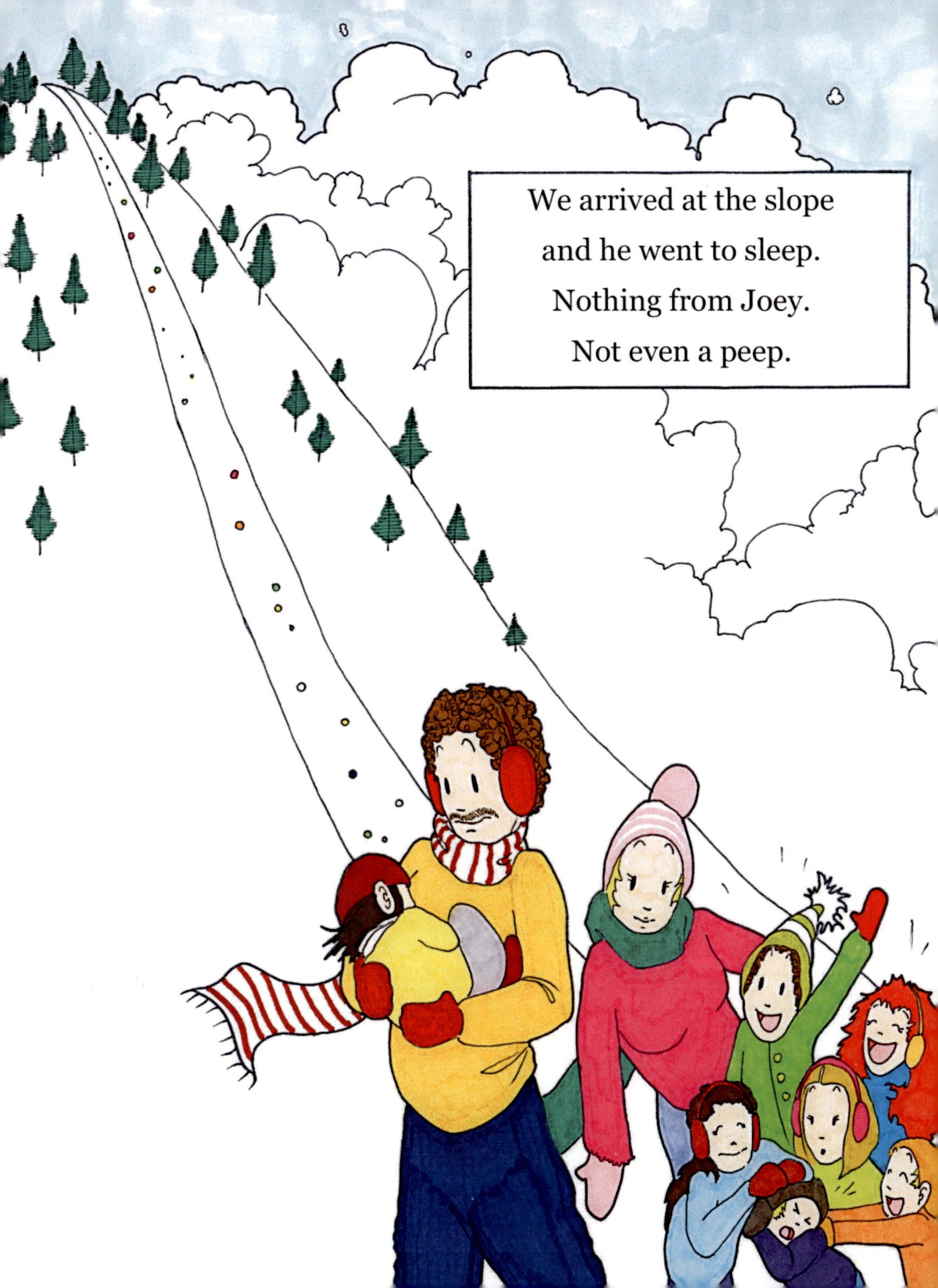

We arrived at the slope
and he went to sleep.
Nothing from Joey.
Not even a peep.

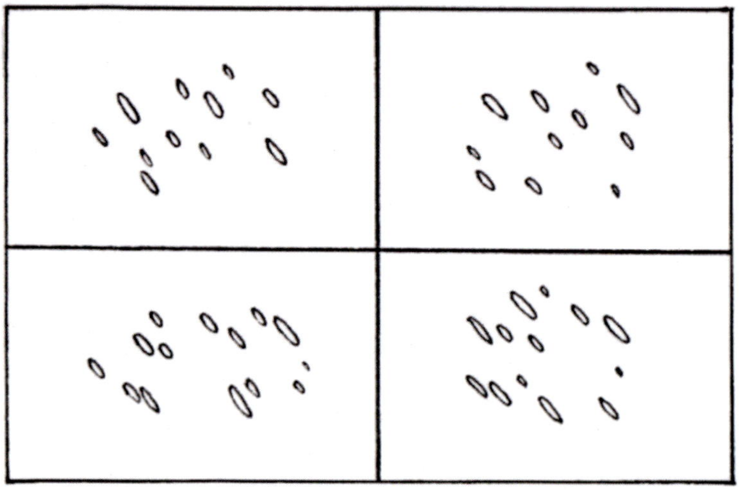

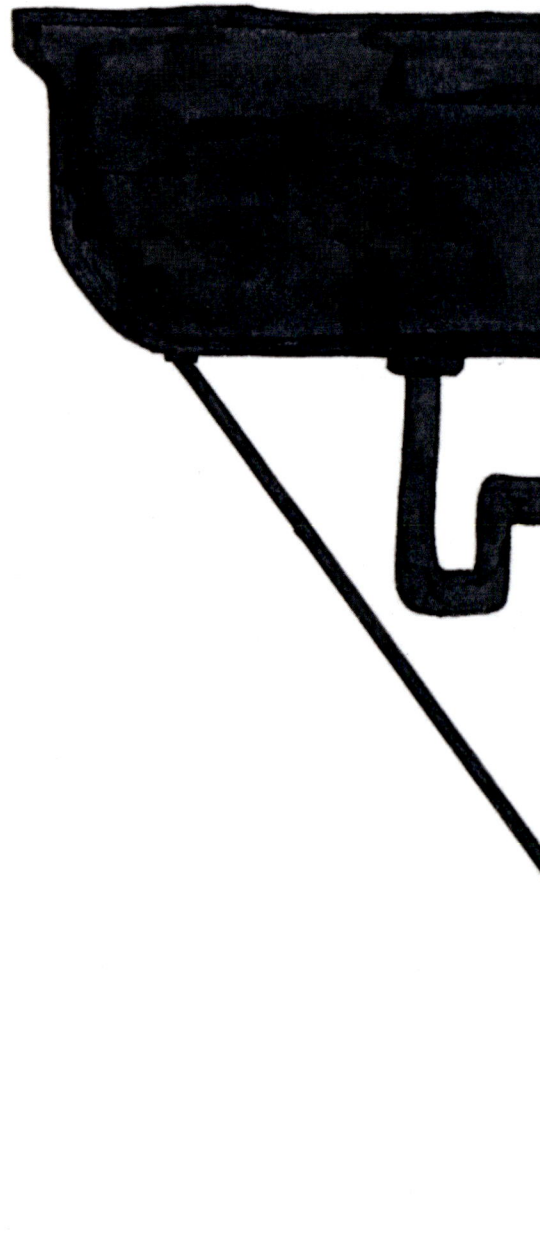

Left Joey alone in his room,
skiing three hours 'til early afternoon.

Z Z Z Z

"Okay" I said to the little guy,
"You want to ski?
Then let's give it a try!

But you have to sit tight
on my shoulder.

No skis now, until you are
older."

He grinned and laughed when we were done,
really loving the snow and sun.

Another time I recall a thoughtful take,
water skiing at some large lake…

He hated that with such a passion,
howling aloud in typical chimp fashion.

In the car cramped with nine together,
this sad fact I do remember:
Joey screaming at all of us,
creating havoc and a really big fuss.

So I put him in the boat that we were towing,
creating great danger without even knowing.
Joey holding on to the boat's steering wheel.
His hand in the air, waving a great deal.

Cars passed us and did a double take,
watching Joey steering like on the lake.

He was so frightened, and I was so mad,
I made a decision that was very bad.

He could have jumped from the boat you see,
and that would have been a catastrophe.
But as luck would have it, he stayed still,
(or really it was God's good will).

Home at night once we were all safe,

I reflected then on my mistake.

Placing little Joey in that dangerous position,

I should have placed my anger in submission.

He summersaulted
all the way to the door,
with all of the kids
watching from the floor.

Every time
the front doorbell rang,
like a cannon
he rolled and banged.

Joey and the kids
summersaulting away,
to open the door in this unusual way.

When my wife shouted at a kid,
this is what little Joey did…

He ran to the one that she was scolding,

bit their finger that he was holding.

He enforced the rules for her demand,
now a child would rush and hide their hand.
Joey diligently following her every rule,
using his bite as the tool.

She tried teaching Joey to eat at the table,
but this was not something he was really able.

Grabbing his food and throwing it fast,
the attempt at teaching quickly did pass.

After a while he became stronger and wild,
not like the past when he was gentle and mild.

One night I came home to see
my wife upset
and crying to me.

Joey got mad and hit her with a stick.

Hearing this occurred, I became sick.

He had then run away, but I didn't know

until I received a call telling me so.

He's at the neighbor's place about a mile away,

I passed that ranch every day.

Off I went to fetch our little guy,

but in my heart I began to cry.

He said,
"Come in and see what I mean!"

The chimp had eaten his
breadbox clean!

He said, "My wife heard a knock
and opened the door -

The chimp ran between her legs
and rolled onto the floor!"

Into the kitchen he went and searched the drawer.
He ate the bread and cookies,
and then searched for more.

But then he just looked at us, seeming so sad,

that I became much less mad.

The next day I borrowed my wife's car.
Wanted to take Joey to see my friend afar.

Just going for a little ride,
Joey as calm as a kitten by my side.

I stopped at my office for only a minute,
returning to see his diaper smeared in it.

On the window and over the seat,
Joey hysterically laughing at his feat.

I wasn't so happy as you might tell,
as diaper doo has a very strong smell.
The windows were now covered with brown.
My spirits dropped all the way down.

For it took an hour to clean his mess,
then find a new diaper for Joey to dress.

My wife, the kids, and I all cried.

I knew I had to quickly decide.

Joey was now a definite danger.

The solution was to give him to a stranger.

On the final day we said goodbye,

all were crying,

I cannot lie.

She drove Joey to meet the circus man,
while I the other way freely ran.

Joey took her hand and looked in her face,
and streams of tears fell all over the place.

We all wept much over this event,
considering all that it meant.

Losing a family member to another life,
not knowing whether for love or strife.

SCHIMPANSE

On a trip to Austria later in life
with all the kids and my wife,
we went to the zoo, a famous place
and headed on over
to the chimpanzee space.

A chimp, aged fifty,
large and unhappy.

He sat in the corner
till I became wacky...

As we ran away fast, I felt so bad,
remembering our Joey,
and feeling so sad.

I thought about this
for awhile.

I couldn't even
break a smile.

For I must have said
something so bad,
that caused
the chimp's anger
to become so mad.

I remember the time he loved those kittens, and
the fun and the joy when he was so smitten.

Now I feared what his suffering might have been.
I immediately knew I had to repent my sin.

Had we known way back when,
the chimp was only a baby then.

Joey was taken away from his mother,
and given then to someone other.

Then I wondered where Joey was now.

If he ever knew why, when, or even how.

Why we sent him so far away.

Our thoughts remain of him to this day.

I can't change Joey's life, I thought,
so onto another way I sought.

To alert all of those
who really want one.

It's not the way...

different things need to be done.

We must stop the harm
to all of them.

Never to capture
or keep in a pen.

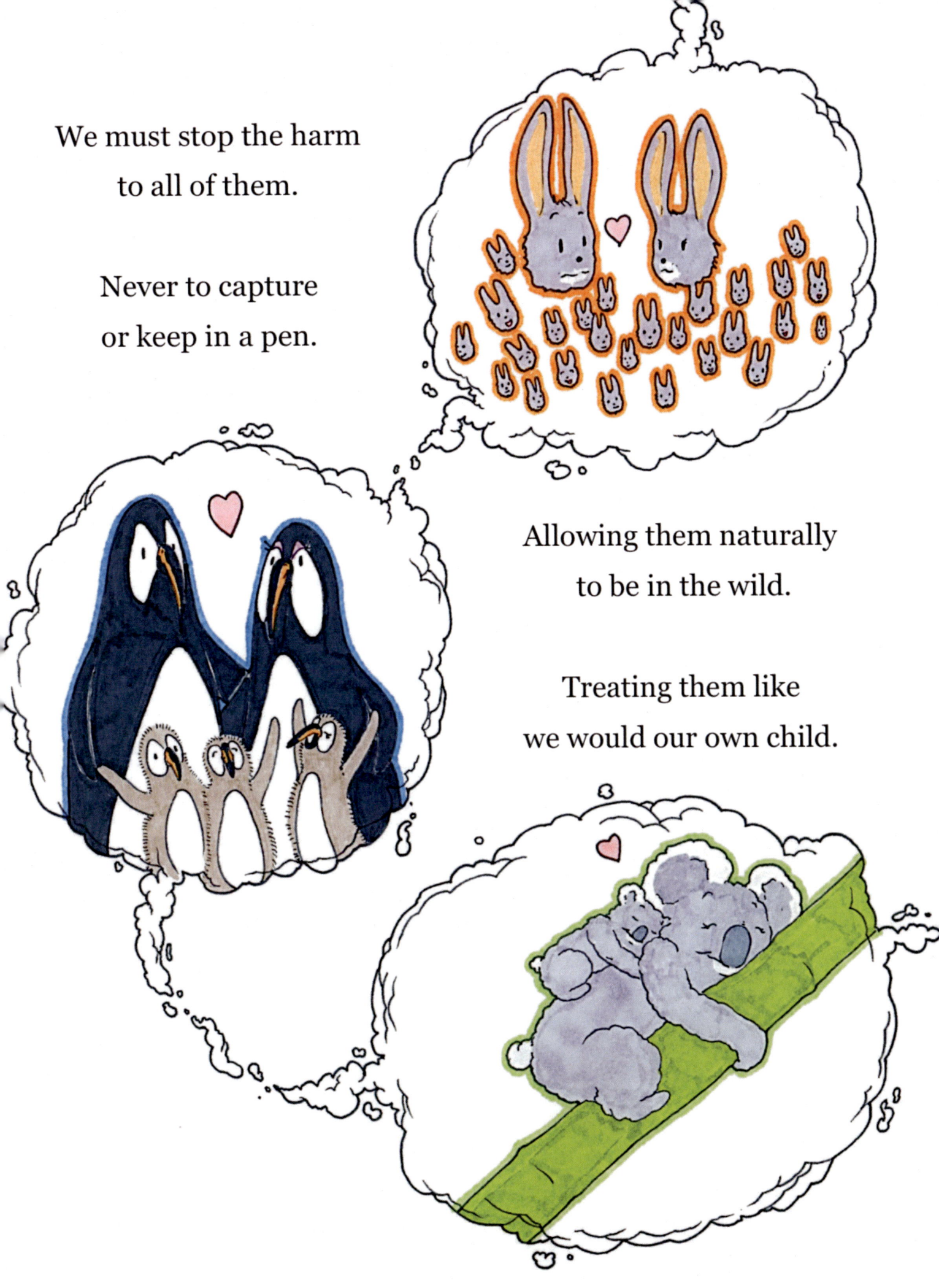

Allowing them naturally
to be in the wild.

Treating them like
we would our own child.

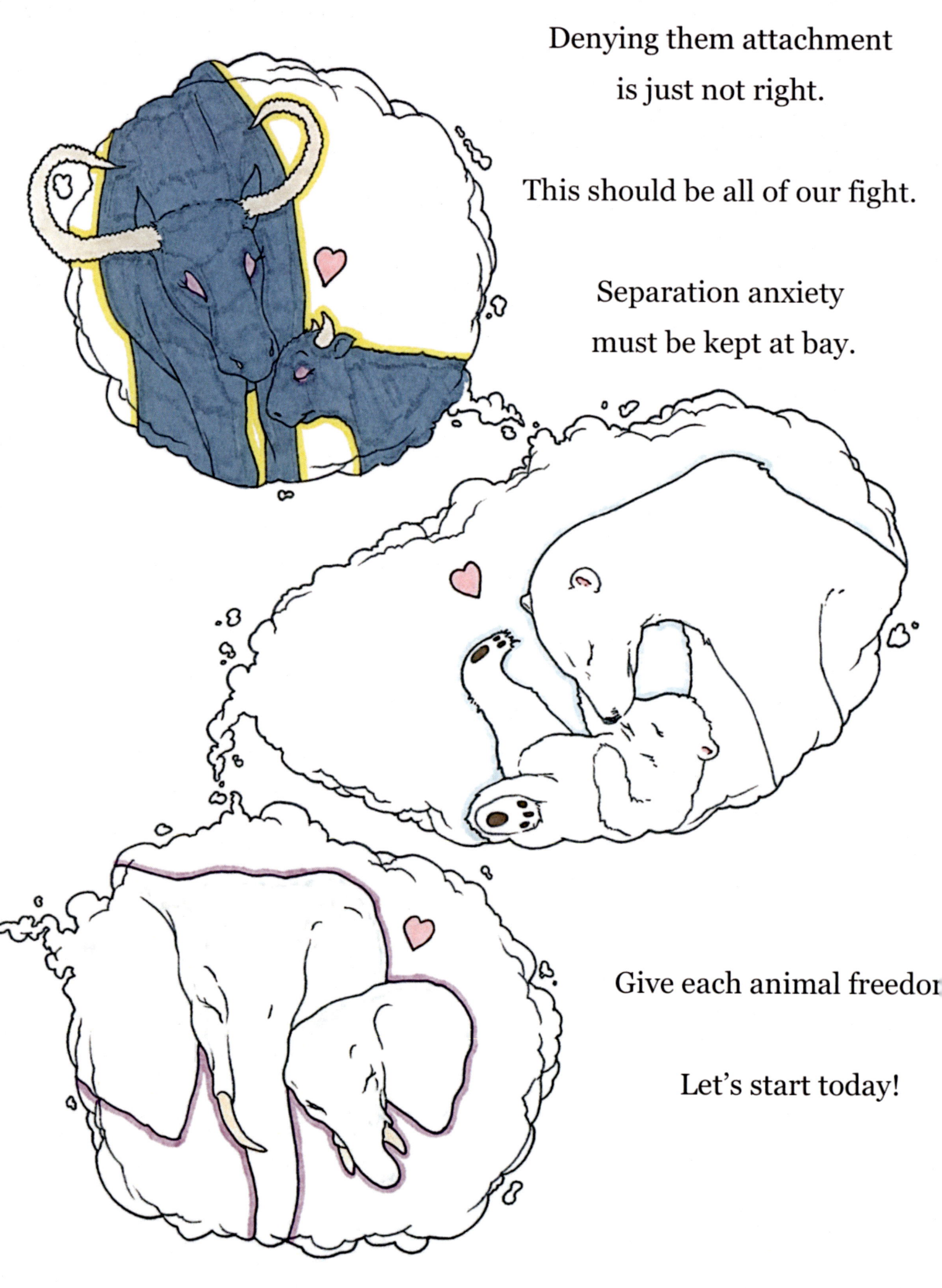

Denying them attachment
is just not right.

This should be all of our fight.

Separation anxiety
must be kept at bay.

Give each animal freedor

Let's start today!

Laws must change to protect each life.

Let's stop their fear, and their strife.

Let animal families stay together.

May it be so forever and ever.

We should always have a great big heart,

and help those who have been kept apart.

Let's help make their shelter and provide

for disrespected animals so they don't have pain inside.

AUTHOR'S NOTE

My initial thought in writing this true story was for children to share in the fun and happiness of our family's adventures with Joey, our adopted baby chimpanzee.

During the writing of this book, while I was recalling my many adventures with Joey, I remembered the happiness I felt during those years. While considering my memories of those events though, I also felt a sense of guilt about how this time ultimately had a negative impact on Joey. While considering his intelligence and loving disposition, I wondered whether he was happy at all, so I began looking at the facts that disturbed me.

When he was removed from his mother as a baby, he suffered separation anxiety that possibly changed his behavior, and then I dislodged him a second time.
Where was he now? Was he happy or sad? Did he even remember his years with our family?

Because of my feelings, I wanted to admit that I had done wrong and accept my responsibility for this act.

The last few pages of our adventure are intended to help children and their parents see the harm in removing any wild animal from their natural habitat and families.

The following pages include actual photos of Joey and my family.

All proceeds from this book will go to primate rescue farms in the United States as well as wildlife support organizations.

Marvin Ginsburg. MD

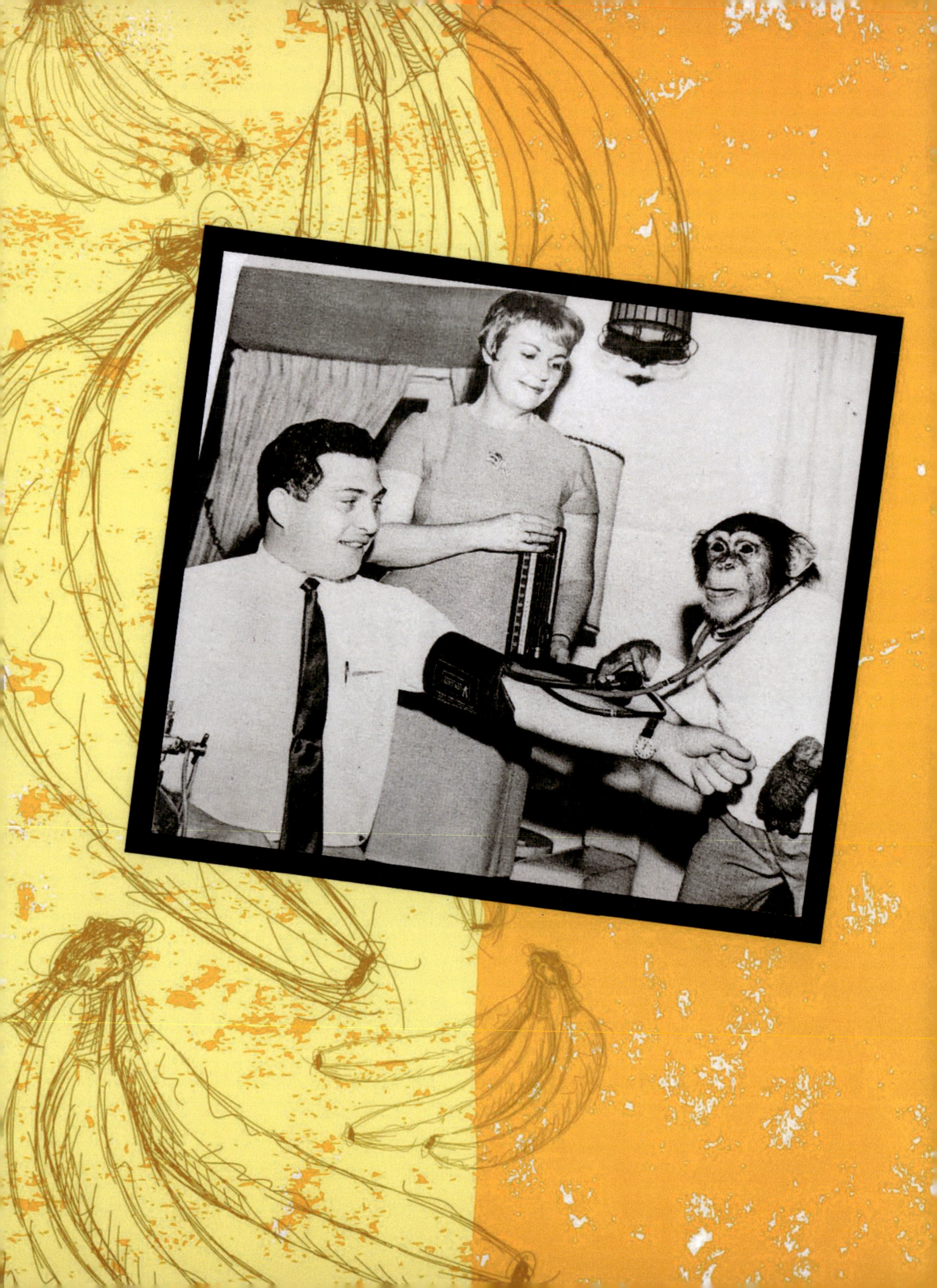